IOANNIS VASILEIOU

ECONOMIC CRISIS, EMPLOYMENT AND SOCIAL AFFAIRS IN THE EUROPEAN UNION

PROPOSALS AND ACTIONS TO COMBAT UNEMPLOYMENT

ATHENS 2019

PUBLISHED IN GREEK BY HISTORICAL QUEST IN 2017

TRANSLATED INTO ENGLISH IN 2019

TRANSLATED BY THE AUTHOR HIMSELF

ART DIRECTOR: SOFIA LIVIERATOU, sofialiv@hotmail.com

ACKNOWLEDGEMENTS
To my beloved Maria Nikou for her
encouragement and moral support

TABLE OF CONTENTS

INTRODUCTION

For more than a few years unemployment has been one of the thorniest problems within the European Union (EU). The recent economic and financial crisis, which has not yet been terminated inevitably raises concerns particularly among young people.

Ever since its establishment, the unremitting battle against unemployment has incontrovertibly been one of the Union's principal priorities. Irrefutably, however, back in the 1950s, nobody could have imagined the current dimensions of this phenomenon, which has indubitably become a scourge with uncertain future consequences.

It is undisputed that since the beginning of the global economic and financial crisis, the Union has been constantly experiencing high unemployment rates coupled with low investment levels. European Commission's fundamental objective is to reverse this situation in order for Europe to be able to recover relatively soon (Europa, 2017; European Commission, 2016; Vasileiou, 2013a, 2014a, 2014b, 2017a, 2017b and 2017c).

It goes without saying that the increase of jobs is of paramount significance but without the creation of a new debt. Such a detail deserves particular attention for quite a few reasons (Europa, 2017; European Commission, 2016; Vasileiou, 2013a, 2014a, 2014b, 2017a, 2017b and 2017c).

We indubitably acknowledge (and this has to be made crystal clear) that numerous significant steps resulting in a variety of beneficial effects have already taken place. This book has been authored with the aim of analyzing, inter alia, the various key Union initiatives and actions in order for unemployment to be rapidly decreased.

Via our meticulous research, we have hitherto drawn the conclusion that the Union is actually heading towards the coveted economic growth, but that does not mean in any way that efforts should be reduced. Although the EU is gradually making progress, a number of member states such as Greece are still facing intense tribulations.

We really hope that these adversities will be diminished in the near future since, otherwise, the consequences will undoubtedly become irreversible with whatever this implies for both member states and the Union as a whole. A functional employment policy will incontrovertibly benefit both the current and the next generation.

Undeniably, social policy is directly linked to employment. Within the present globalized society, issues related to the tremendously sensitive area of "social protection and inclusion" are of vital importance and are characterized by a particularly multidimensional impact on international developments.

It goes without saying that the EU has indeed managed to come up with a satisfactory range of strategies and policies. These are being rigorously analyzed in the following chapters.

The aim of the book is twofold. We attempt on the one hand to critically present the entire spectrum of the Union's actions in the context of these neuralgic issues in a simplified and comprehensive manner and, on the other hand, to point out that solutions for a more optimistic tomorrow indeed exist as far as, of course, specific conditions and prerequisites apply.

This book is based, among other things, on the critical scrutiny of several articles by some of the foremost authors and scholars worldwide. These articles have been published in scientific journals of major significance and aim at a deeper understanding in order for a number of constructive conclusions to be efficaciously drawn.

The scholars' names unambiguously reveal the quality and scientific validity of the articles: Agell, Alexiou, Allin, Bambra, Bartolomew, Bentolila, Blanchflower, Brine, Büchel, Calmfors, Christodoulakis, Coombes, Daveri, Dieckhoff, Ederveen, Eikemo, Feld, Fialová, Fragoulis, Gobbin, Heinrich, Hildebrand, Huizinga, Janáčková, Kazamaki Ottersten, Kelleher, Kinsella (Ray and Maurice), Klenha, Kogan, Lipsmeyer, Livanos, Mahler, Mamatzakis, Masson, Moore, Nahuis, Newell, Núñez, Öster, Overman, Palazuelos-Martinez, Parikh, Pastore, Petrongolo, Pissarides, Pollmann-Schult, Pratschke, Puga, Raybould, Schneider, Scott, Shadforth, Smith (Fred), Smith (Jennifer C.), Stanef, Stewart, Sweeney, Tabellini, Tatsiramos, Taylor, Vandenbussche, Van Aarle, Vintrová, Walsh, Welbers, Wozniak, Zamfir and Zhu.

Apart from the introduction, the book comprises four additional chapters. In Chapter 1, titled *"Economic Crisis, Employment, Growth and Investments: A Brief Analysis"*, we attempt to methodically focus on a) how the global economic and financial crisis affected the EU in the three aforesaid sectors and b) what is exactly included within the sector of employment and social affairs.

From quite a few studies we have examined in the recent past, we have actually realized that both the concept and the content of this area are slightly "abstract" and in more than a few cases the clarification provided is far from being considered as sufficient, at least in our opinion.

Our dominant aim is for the reader to become familiar with the precise meaning of the term "employment and social affairs" in a simple language and avoiding any abstruse details which are highly probable to lead to confusion and misunderstandings.

We are convinced that the best possible understanding will lead the reader to a more profound delving into the subject and will enable him to realize why this area is so closely linked to the economic and financial crisis and why it continuously affects so many people.

In Chapter 2, the *"European Union Funding Programs for Employment and Social Affairs"* are being painstakingly scrutinized. More specifically, we concentrate on the European Social Fund, the European Globalization Adjustment Fund, the Fund for European Aid to the most Deprived and the "EU Programme for Employment and Social Innovation".

In Chapter 3, a detailed analysis of *"The Foremost European Union Institutions and Bodies for Employment and Social Affairs"* takes place. In particular, the role of the European Parliament, the Council of the EU, the European Commission, the European Economic and Social Committee, the Committee of the Regions and the European Investment Bank is being methodically examined.

Additionally, we refer to specific EU agencies which play a pivotal role within the context of employment and social affairs. The abovementioned spectrum is incontrovertibly multifarious, but we imagine that through our analysis difficulties in terms of understanding will not be too many.

Finally, in Chapter 4, the principal *"Concluding Remarks"* are being drawn in order for the main points to be satisfactorily summarized. In the context of this chapter, the already achieved objectives are being methodically highlighted, the existing problems are being meticulously analyzed and the future prospects are being painstakingly examined. We remain optimistic that the conclusions' chapter will indeed provide the reader with impetus for further study and research.

CHAPTER 1

ECONOMIC CRISIS, EMPLOYMENT, GROWTH AND INVESTMENTS: A BRIEF ANALYSIS

The impact of the global economic and financial crisis has been incontrovertibly devastating, affecting almost all areas of the social and politicoeconomic sphere. It would be impossible for the EU to remain unaffected. Some of its member states are still being tortured and Greece is the most characteristic example. Regrettably, in that country the crisis continues and nobody knows when and under what circumstances it will be terminated (Pelagidis and Mitsopoulos, 2014; Vasileiou, 2013a, 2014a, 2014b, 2017a, 2017b and 2017c).

As it was expected, the crisis led to tremendously high unemployment rates and outstandingly low investment levels in the Union. In simple terms, we note that in the short term, low levels of investment diminish economic growth due to the fact that they result in reduced economic activity. In the long run, however, the low investment level's impact is even more serious, since it noticeably affects both the competitiveness and the economy's growth potential (Europa, 2017; European Commission, 2016; Vasileiou, 2013a, 2014a, 2014b, 2017a, 2017b and 2017c).

Numerous influential scholars worldwide have conducted extended research on unemployment, its various implications and its relevant areas, such as economic growth, globalization, regional disparities, taxation, education (combined with lifelong learning), criminality, labor market reforms, industrial restructuring, immigration, social welfare policies and the role of domestic political institutions.

In particular, Blanchflower and Shadforth (2009) attempt to systematically link unemployment with migration, while Sweeney (1994) discusses the impact of long-term unemployment. Calmfors (2001) meticulously focuses on unemployment, not in an abstract way, but in close combination with labor market reforms and the Monetary Union.

Núñez and Livanos (2010) try to associate higher education with unemployment in the EU-15. More specifically, in their article they conclude that, in general, higher education indeed increases employment chances. Nonetheless, the impact of the university degree on the issue of avoiding long-term unemployment is lower.

By attempting a critical comparison, the two authors find that at EU-15 level, the impact of higher education on short-term unemployment is more pronounced than that on long-term one. This is explained by the fact that the university degree is considered to be more important in the early years of the professional career.

Diversifications were also observed at national level, which is quite reasonable. In particular, in the United Kingdom, Belgium and Finland, the authors observed that the impact of higher education on employment (in relation to short-term unemployment) was indeed significant.

On the contrary, in the cases of Greece, Italy and Portugal, the degree holder had difficulty in finding a job, and it is particularly interesting that similar conclusions were also drawn for countries characterized by internationally recognized higher education systems (Germany, Sweden, France and Luxembourg). In our opinion, such a finding should be a matter of serious concern.

Lipsmeyer and Zhu (2011) methodically concentrate on immigration, globalization and unemployment benefits in developed EU states. They critically delve into the way according to which global economic forces have an effect on welfare policies in industrialized states. Their dominant pursuit is the accomplishment of a satisfactory analysis of the impact of immigration flow resulting from globalization. According to the two scholars, within the Union, the issue of immigration and unemployment compensation is more related to domestic political pressures than to the market forces of integration and the opening of borders.

Mahler et al. (2000) analyze in three levels (individual, regional and national) the link between economics and public support in the Union. Overman et al. (2002) describe the unemployment clusters in European countries and regions, while Stanef (2012) attempts the (admittedly difficult and extremely complicated) measuring of differences between employment in urban and rural areas. Daveri et al. (2000), using a critical and outstandingly systematic method, refer to the way of "linking" unemployment, growth and taxation in industrial countries.

Alexiou (2001) has carried out a tremendously significant study, in the context of which he is based on a Post Keynesian macroeconomic framework to provide a satisfactory explanation for unemployment in Europe. Alexiou provides evidence in terms of unemployment in the Union's member states using econometric models. The results of this study practically strengthen the view that aggregate-demand policies can actually have significant impact on the employed population of a region or a country.

We deliberately avoided proceeding into a deeper analysis of the econometric methods, since this book is not only for economists and perhaps econometric analyses may complicate some of the readers. However, we can only praise Alexiou's effort, as through his analysis he manages to provide a complete picture of such a burning issue.

Bartolomew et al. (1995) and Smith (2011) attempt a measurement of unemployment and its consequences in general in the United Kingdom, while Kinsella and Kinsella (2011) and Walsh (2000) focus on the case of Ireland. Coombes and Raybould (2004) critically concentrate on unemployment in England, based on the 2001 census.

Kazamaki Ottersten (2004) focuses on the particular noteworthiness of lifelong learning and how it is directly related to employability. Concurrently, she conducts a critical examination on precisely how European labor markets are linked to lifelong learning, with particular emphasis on the role of the European Investment Bank (EIB).

We notice that Kazamaki Ottersten indeed raises an extremely critical issue, as these days employment opportunities are indeed subject to constant changes. This issue was literally "burning" in 2004, when her article was published, so we can easily understand its even higher significance in the current period.

Ederveen et al. (2007) deal with the relationship between labor mobility and regional disparities in the Union, concentrating on the particular role of female labor participation. These authors underline the fact that significant differences in terms of unemployment rates and income per capita within the EU can incontrovertibly be observed. Nonetheless, they believe that labor mobility in general can indeed contribute to the reduction of regional disparities.

Bambra and Eikemo (2009) critically focus on the existing link between unemployment, welfare state regimes and health. In particular, they perform a tremendously interesting comparative study in terms of the relationship between unemployment and self-reported health in 23 European countries.

Christodoulakis and Mamatzakis (2009) systematically cope with the assessment of economic forecasts in the Union, while Feld (2005) refers to the notable European Constitution Project from the Constitutional Political Economy perspective.

Gobbin and Van Aarle (2001) painstakingly scrutinize the noteworthiness of fiscal adjustments in terms of the always complex and multidimensional transition to the Economic and Monetary Union.

Pollmann-Schult and Büchel (2005) critically delve into the tremendously significant issues of unemployment benefits, the duration of unemployment and the subsequent job quality in West Germany, while Kogan (2004) rigorously examines the unemployment dynamics of male immigrants in Germany.

Öster and Agell (2007) investigate the relationship between unemployment and crime in Sweden, which is a particularly sensitive issue, requiring maximum attention, while Petrongolo and Pissarides (2008) attempt a remarkable comparative analysis of unemployment in the United Kingdom, France and Spain.

Stewart (2005) successfully deals with another tremendously significant issue on which numerous scholars have actually focused. In reality do unemployment rates and the Gross Domestic Product (GDP) rationally reflect prosperity levels in the Union's regions? Do numbers really tell the truth, or mislead? It goes without saying that numbers indeed provide an insight into the economic situation. If, for example, in a region the unemployment rate is exceedingly high, no prosperity exists.

In our opinion, numbers partly reveal the truth, but for a complete picture it is necessary to take into account other factors as well, such as the distribution of wealth. Furthermore, it is essential to analyze both the political and sociological aspects which characterize that particular region. "Prosperity" at economic level is directly influenced by the political situation of that particular time, so a synthesis of data and conclusions may actually provide a satisfactory response.

Tatsiramos (2009) refers to the key issue of unemployment insurance in Europe, while critically focusing not only on the unemployment duration but also on the subsequent employment stability. Scott and Kelleher (1996) methodically deal with the burning issue of vocational training in the Union.

Dieckhoff (2011) conducts a highly interesting comparative analysis between Austria, Denmark, Spain and the United Kingdom, with the aim of drawing a number of fruitful conclusions in terms of the impact of unemployment on the subsequent job quality in Europe. Fialová and Schneider (2009) focus on labor market institutions and their impact on labor market performance in the New Member Countries of the Union.

Palazuelos-Martinez (2007) emphasizes the structure and evolution of trade in Central and Eastern Europe in the 1990s, while Vintrová (2004) attempts to delve into a scrupulous investigation with regard to the route of Central and East European countries in order to join the Union. She underlines the various adjustment problems, the outstandingly critical institutional adjustment and miscellaneous noteworthy issues related to real and nominal convergence.

Janáčková (1998) refers to the multidimensional challenges the Czech Monetary Policy faced in terms of its intense effort to eventually achieve the coveted convergence so as to successfully enter the Union.

Newell and Pastore (2006) methodically focus on the sensitive issues of regional unemployment and industrial restructuring in Poland. It goes without saying that such topics are extremely interesting and are indeed characterized by quite a few attention-grabbing implications.

Fragoulis et al. (2004) critically concentrate on the particular notability of the functional and fruitful improvement of opportunities and perspectives for adult learning at the then acceding and candidate countries of Central and Eastern Europe.

In general, at that particular era, numerous scholars had indeed focused on the issues of education and institutional adaptation of the acceding countries of Central and Eastern Europe, as everybody was wondering whether their EU accession would take place smoothly and without major difficulties and delays.

As we can easily conclude, unemployment, combined with economic growth and the calamitous economic and financial crisis, has been at the heart of thoughts and debates, not only among scholars, but among all thinking citizens regardless of age, gender or scientific training.

The data listed in the following paragraphs shed light on a number of interesting and perhaps unknown facts.

In January 2008, there were 16.1 million unemployed in the Union, which means 6.8% of working population. Five years later (January 2013), the number of unemployed had reached 26.4 million, or 10.9% of working population (Europa, 2017; European Commission, 2016; European Commission/Coordination, 2017; European Commission/Social Protection and Social Inclusion, 2017; Vasileiou, 2013a, 2014a, 2014b, 2017a, 2017b and 2017c).

In May 2016, the unemployed in the EU were 21 million (8.6% of working population) of which four million young people. The youth unemployment rate reached 18.6% (Europa, 2017; European Commission, 2016; European Commission/Social Protection and Social Inclusion, 2017; Vasileiou, 2013a, 2014a, 2014b, 2017a, 2017b and 2017c).

According to official European Commission figures of October 2016, the annual level of investment was approximately €300 bn lower than in the past. Such an element deserves particular attention as it reveals a tremendously negative trend (Europa, 2017; European Commission, 2016).

However, it should be noted that despite the fact that money was indeed available, investment eventually remained low for the simple reason that investors did not (and some still don't have) the confidence to invest (Europa, 2017; European Commission, 2016; European Commission/Coordination, 2017; Vasileiou, 2013a, 2014a, 2014b, 2017a, 2017b and 2017c).

Inevitably, the fluidity of the situation gives rise to an increased uncertainty, particularly taking into account the fact that a number of the Union's economies are characterized, inter alia, by high public and private debt (Europa, 2017; European Commission, 2016; European Commission/Coordination, 2017; Vasileiou, 2013a, 2014a, 2014b, 2017a, 2017b and 2017c).

In addition to that, receiving grants or loans remains problematic in quite a few countries, especially for small and medium-sized companies. Furthermore, we must add that governments indeed cut back on investment because of public debt which rose from an average of 60% of the Union's GDP in 2008 to about 90% in 2015 (Europa, 2017; European Commission, 2016; European Commission/Social Protection and Social Inclusion, 2017).

Such an increase incontrovertibly results in awe and we are really wondering on the one hand if the EU actually foresaw the impact of the crisis and, on the other hand, in the case it had foreseen it, if it could be more satisfactorily prepared in order to avoid or at least mitigate all those dreadful consequences (Alexiou, 2001; Bambra and Eikemo, 2009; Blanchflower and Shadforth, 2009; Calmfors, 2001; Christodoulakis and Mamatzakis, 2009;

Daveri et al., 2000; Dieckhoff, 2011; Ederveen et al., 2007; Feld, 2005; Fialová and Schneider, 2009; Gobbin and Van Aarle, 2001; Heinrich and Hildebrand, 2005; Kazamaki Ottersten, 2004; Lipsmeyer and Zhu, 2011; Núñez and Livanos, 2010; Overman et al., 2002; Stanef, 2012; Stewart, 2005; Tatsiramos, 2009).

The necessity for an immediate readjustment of certain policies was evident. Following quite a few intensified studies, the European Commission decided that the ideal handling of the situation required a systematic focus on a) the reinvigoration of investments, b) a more functional and far more efficient continuation of market reforms and c) the fastest possible implementation of adequate financial policies, seeking to avoid an excessively high public debt (Europa, 2017; European Commission, 2016; European Commission/Coordination, 2017; Vasileiou, 2013a, 2014a, 2014b, 2017a, 2017b and 2017c).

And, in our opinion, it did the right thing, since these three components undoubtedly constituted the "hot potato" for both the economic present and future of the already tortured by the crisis Union.

The European Commission, together with the EIB, launched the investment plan for Europe which meticulously focuses on a) the efficient use of both existing and new financial resources, b) the rapid removal of the various barriers to investment and c) the effective provision of visibility and technical assistance to investment projects (Europa, 2017; European Commission, 2016; European Commission/Social Protection and Social Inclusion, 2017).

Attention must also be paid to the fact that in 2015 a European Fund for Strategic Investments (EFSI) was established with an initial €21 bn "backed" by the Union (Europa, 2017; European Commission, 2016).

On the basis of the Commission's data of October 2016, this will be increased due to the "multiplier effect" which will become a reality by the coveted attraction of public and private investors who will trigger investments of more than €315 bn over a period of three years (Europa, 2017; European Commission, 2016).

According to the same figures, after one year this plan was expected to mobilize more than €138 bn for new investments all over the Union, not only from big companies but also from local small and medium-sized ones. The Commission committed itself to a doubling of the fund and actually proposed to raise the target to at least €500 bn by 2020, with a commitment to double it to €630 bn by 2022 at the latest. Such a detail must under no circumstances go unnoticed (Europa, 2017; European Commission, 2016; European Commission/Social Protection and Social Inclusion, 2017).

EFSI's momentousness and outstandingly pivotal role literally obliges us to further delve into its foremost initiatives and actions.

EFSI is responsible for providing guarantees for the support of EIB-funded projects and focuses on innovation, infrastructure and smaller companies. In practice, we would argue that EFSI provides a guarantee, thus making the EIB capable of investing a) into a greater amount of projects, some of which are considered to be of "higher risk" and b) much sooner than without the guarantee (Europa, 2017; European Commission, 2016; Vasileiou, 2013a, 2014a, 2014b, 2017a, 2017b and 2017c).

EFSI's foremost pursuit was the mobilization of at least €315 bn in additional investments in the real economy by the middle of 2018. Furthermore, according to the same data, EFSI is active in 27 member states and is highly probable to trigger over €138 bn in investment, based on the approved financing by October 2016 (Europa, 2017; European Commission, 2016; European Commission/Coordination, 2017; Vasileiou, 2013a, 2014a, 2014b, 2017a, 2017b and 2017c).

It in indeed worth mentioning that, by October 2016, under the EFSI, 134 infrastructure projects had already been approved. These actually represented financing of €17.4 bn, which is not at all insignificant. Apart from that, more than 220 financing agreements worth €7.5 bn were approved for smaller companies, which is indeed remarkable, as businesses of this size need special support and can incontrovertibly contribute a great deal towards growth. From this finance, around 290,000 smaller companies are expected to benefit in a sufficient manner and such a figure is indeed noteworthy especially nowadays (Europa, 2017; European Commission, 2016; European Commission/Coordination, 2017; Vasileiou, 2013a, 2014a, 2014b, 2017a, 2017b and 2017c).

What is more, special emphasis must be placed on Ginkgo Fund 2, which is a tremendously important project for cleaning up contaminated industrial sites and transforming them into offices and homes. Always according to Commission's data of October 2016, this remarkable project may create approximately 5,000 housing units and 8,500 jobs in France and Belgium (Europa, 2017; European Commission, 2016; Vasileiou, 2013a, 2014a, 2014b, 2017a, 2017b and 2017c).

EIB financing under the EFSI amounts to €30 million, while we must point out that the support from the EFSI actually managed to attract private investors in order to meet the entire cost of the project, which was €120 million. Furthermore, attention must be paid to the fact that, without exaggeration, the decontamination that takes place through Ginkgo is of vital significance, since 3.5 million former industrial sites remain vacant (Europa, 2017; European Commission, 2016; Vasileiou, 2013a, 2014a, 2014b, 2017a, 2017b and 2017c). This is another significant piece of evidence that EU policies on these issues are indeed successful and undeniably provide guarantees towards a more heartening future.

In addition to financing, the investment plan includes specific and tremendously useful tools created by the Union to provide noteworthy assistance in order for the various benefits of investment projects to be channeled into the real economy (Europa, 2017; European Commission, 2016; European Commission/Coordination, 2017; Vasileiou, 2013a, 2014a, 2014b, 2017a, 2017b and 2017c).

In September 2015, the European Investment Advisory Hub was successfully established with the aim to provide technical and administrative support to project promoters in Europe (Europa, 2017; European Commission, 2016; European Commission/ Social Protection and Social Inclusion, 2017; Vasileiou, 2013a, 2014a, 2014b, 2017a, 2017b and 2017c).

We meticulously focus on the fact that not only the abovementioned promoters, but also private companies and public authorities can indeed receive technical support, which will provide them with notable assistance in order to attract investment interest (a parameter of paramount importance) and to actually initiate their projects (Europa, 2017; European Commission, 2016; European Commission/Coordination, 2017; Vasileiou, 2013a, 2014a, 2014b, 2017a, 2017b and 2017c).

We must not forget that, additionally, they will have the opportunity to receive specific and outstandingly valuable advice on the most appropriate sources of funding and also to have access to a unique range of financial and technical expertise, which is a truly remarkable fact since it will generously offer enormous facilitation in a wide range of issues (Europa, 2017; European Commission, 2016; Vasileiou, 2013a, 2014a, 2014b, 2017a, 2017b and 2017c).

Concomitantly, the European Investment Project Portal is another significant creation of the Commission with the target to provide investors with a clearer and infinitely more complete picture of the investment opportunities in the Union. The European Investment Project Portal was launched on June 1, 2016, and is considered to be a decisive step towards a rapid economic recovery (Europa, 2017; European Commission, 2016; European Commission/Social Protection and Social Inclusion, 2017; Vasileiou, 2013a, 2014a, 2014b, 2017a, 2017b and 2017c).

The European Structural and Investment Funds (European Regional Development Fund, European Social Fund, Cohesion Fund, European Agricultural Fund for Rural Development and European Maritime and Fisheries Fund) play their own unique role towards the Union's fast economic development.

For the period 2014-20, these funds together have a budget of €454 bn and invest in a variety of neuralgic areas, such as a) support for smaller companies, b) research, development and innovation, c) information and communication technologies and d) low-carbon economy (Europa, 2017; European Commission, 2016; Vasileiou, 2013a, 2014a, 2014b, 2017a, 2017b and 2017c).

To avoid misunderstandings, it is emphasized that the structural funds differ from the EFSI and this difference lies precisely in the fact that they finance projects through grants and financial instruments and are implemented in a "decentralized" manner in the member states. On the contrary, the EFSI actually provides risk financing instruments through the EIB (Europa, 2017; European Commission, 2016; Vasileiou, 2013a, 2014a, 2014b, 2017a, 2017b and 2017c).

Apart from that, it is worth mentioning that any project that a) is actually considered to be economically viable, b) is in line with the Union's priorities for investment and c) can contribute to employment and growth in the Union, may be eligible for funding by both the structural funds and the EFSI (Europa, 2017; European Commission, 2016; Vasileiou, 2013a, 2014a, 2014b, 2017a, 2017b and 2017c).

We irrefutably claim that the abovementioned data reveal a mature and detailed planning. Achieving these goals will certainly result in a better tomorrow for the Union and its citizens.

The area of employment and social affairs is absolutely vital for both the EU present and future. It is true that responsibility for employment and social policy lies primarily with national governments. The Union's funding practically supports and in a sense "complements" their efforts in general (Europa, 2017; European Commission, 2016; Vasileiou, 2013a, 2014a, 2014b, 2017a, 2017b and 2017c).

We surely welcome the fact that the EU is in the forefront as regards the key issue of efficaciously tackling the consequences of population ageing (Europa, 2017; European Commission, 2016; European Commission/Social Protection and Social Inclusion, 2017; Vasileiou, 2013a, 2014a, 2014b, 2017a, 2017b and 2017c).

That is why both the Union's social and employment policy directly aim at a) the sufficient protection of disabled people, b) the facilitation of the (particularly problematic in some cases) transition from school to work, c) the best possible assistance to find a job, which is outstandingly difficult these days, d) the immediate modernization with regard to social security systems, e) poverty reduction and f) a further facilitation in terms of the free movement of workers all over the Union (Europa,

2017; European Commission, 2016; European Commission/ Coordination, 2017; European Commission/Social Protection and Social Inclusion, 2017).

What is more, the Union a) closely monitors and coordinates national policies, b) enhances and actively supports entrepreneurship, training and skills development in a methodical way, c) continuously encourages member states to constructively exchange best practices with regard to the burning issues of pensions, social inclusion and the ceaseless fight against poverty and d) makes laws on workers' rights, discrimination at work and the efficacious coordination of social security schemes, while simultaneously monitoring their implementation (Europa, 2017; European Commission, 2016; Vasileiou, 2013a, 2014a, 2014b, 2017a, 2017b and 2017c).

In addition to employment, the employment and social affairs sector includes tremendously noteworthy subcategories relating to a) workers' rights, b) social security and inclusion, c) skills and d) working and living abroad (Europa, 2017; European Commission, 2016; European Commission/Social Protection and Social Inclusion, 2017).

With regard to employment, the European Commission methodically focuses on four (equally significant) principal components. In particular, it systematically encourages national governments to a) strive to reduce inequalities in terms of the labor market, b) monitor as closely as possible the employment policies in the Union's member states, c) create job opportunities and d) adequately support economic competitiveness (Europa, 2017; European Commission, 2016; European Commission/ Coordination, 2017).

As regards workers' rights, it is worth noting that EU laws towards a) combating discrimination in the most effective way, b) limiting (always in a reasonable context) working hours, c) encouraging, promoting and enhancing safer working conditions and d) guaranteeing that workers receive adequate compensation for work injuries, already exist (Europa, 2017; European Commission, 2016).

As far as the particularly sensitive issue of social security and inclusion is concerned, the Union has also been properly prepared. Hence, it successfully provides and coordinates funding with the aim of satisfactorily supporting member states to a) invest in human resources in areas such as the assistance for finding a job, training, healthcare, childcare and infrastructure accessibility and b) achieve the best possible reforms with regard to the outstandingly neuralgic social security systems (Europa, 2017; European Commission, 2016).

Via our hitherto conducted research, we are indeed in position to conclude that the Commission is constantly encouraging, supporting and complementing member states' policies in the areas of social protection and social inclusion (Europa, 2017; European Commission, 2016; European Commission/Social Protection and Social Inclusion, 2017; Vasileiou, 2013a, 2014a, 2015 and 2017b).

In line with the Europe 2020 strategy, the fundamental objectives are a) the exit from poverty and social exclusion of at least 20 million people and b) the increase to 75% of the employment of 20-64 year olds (Europa, 2017; European Commission, 2016; European Commission/Social Protection and Social Inclusion, 2017; Vasileiou, 2013a, 2014a, 2015 and 2017b).

If these indubitably significant goals are accomplished, this will be a colossal achievement especially nowadays. However, even in the case that full achievement fails, nobody can blame the Union either for sloppiness or lack of effort (Alexiou, 2001; Bambra and Eikemo, 2009; Blanchflower and Shadforth, 2009; Calmfors, 2001; Christodoulakis and Mamatzakis, 2009; Daveri et al., 2000; Dieckhoff, 2011; Ederveen et al., 2007; Feld, 2005; Fialová and Schneider, 2009; Gobbin and Van Aarle, 2001; Heinrich and Hildebrand, 2005; Kazamaki Ottersten, 2004; Lipsmeyer and Zhu, 2011; Núñez and Livanos, 2010; Overman et al., 2002; Stanef, 2012; Stewart, 2005; Tatsiramos, 2009).

Both the Agenda for New Skills and Jobs and the Platform against Poverty and Social Exclusion are first-class initiatives of "Europe 2020" for a more optimistic future (Europa, 2017; European Commission, 2016; European Commission/Social Protection and Social Inclusion, 2017; Vasileiou, 2013a, 2014a, 2015 and 2017b).

It goes without saying that another outstandingly significant factor is the Social Investment Package, through which the Commission manages to provide satisfactory guidance to member states with the aims of a) a lifelong social investment and b) the best possible updating as regards their (often neuralgic) social welfare systems (Europa, 2017; European Commission, 2016; European Commission/Social Protection and Social Inclusion, 2017; Vasileiou, 2013a, 2014a, 2015 and 2017b).

Furthermore, it is essential to point out that the package actually complements a) the White Paper on Pensions, b) the Employment Package and c) the Youth Employment Package (Europa, 2017; European Commission, 2016; European Commission/Social Protection and Social Inclusion, 2017; Vasileiou, 2013a, 2014a, 2015 and 2017b).

What is more, special attention must be paid to the equally noteworthy European Semester. This essentially provides a specific framework for monitoring and steering not only the economic, but also the social reforms in member states in order for the "Europe 2020" targets to be satisfactorily (and rapidly) accomplished (Europa, 2017; European Commission, 2016; European Commission/Social Protection and Social Inclusion, 2017; Vasileiou, 2013a, 2014a, 2015 and 2017b).

We must also mention that not only the challenges and the miscellaneous relevant issues, but also the proposed solutions are clearly included within the context of the notable Country-specific Recommendations (Europa, 2017; European Commission, 2016; European Commission/Social Protection and Social Inclusion, 2017; Vasileiou, 2013a, 2014a, 2015 and 2017b).

Moreover, another critical component is the fact that the European Commission engages in a close (and particularly constructive) cooperation with member states via the Social Protection Committee, constantly striving to achieve the rational use of the "Open Method of Co-ordination" in pivotal areas such as healthcare, long-term care, social inclusion and pensions ("social Open Method of Co-ordination") (Europa, 2017; European Commission, 2016; European Commission/ Social Protection and Social Inclusion, 2017; Vasileiou, 2013a, 2014a, 2015 and 2017b).

We argue that this "social Open Method of Co-ordination" is practically a voluntary political cooperation process according on the one hand to specific agreed common goals and on the other hand to the precise progress measurement for the fast accomplishment of such goals[1]. It is only natural that this process requires close and sufficient cooperation with stakeholders such as the civil society and social partners (Europa, 2017; European Commission, 2016; European Commission/Social Protection and Social Inclusion, 2017; Vasileiou, 2013a, 2014a, 2015 and 2017b).

The outstandingly critical issue of skills becomes sufficiently complex since the adequate qualifications and skills which are required in order to find a job constantly change over the years, due to the unremitting progress of science and technology (Europa, 2017; European Commission, 2016; Vasileiou, 2013a, 2014a, 2014b, 2017a, 2017b and 2017c).

---

1. *Based on common indicators.*

Technology has substituted man in a wide range of jobs and this has a positive and a negative side. Speed and economic benefits especially on production issues have incontrovertibly exploded, but on the other hand the nightmarish scourge of unemployment is constantly on the rise.

Through its truly multidimensional activities, the EU strives a) to contribute to a substantial development of these skills, b) to accomplish an efficient management of the availability of required skills, with a view to preventing any mismatches and c) towards a methodical facilitation of the formal recognition of qualifications abroad so that citizens can live, study and work anywhere in Europe (Europa, 2017; European Commission, 2016; Vasileiou, 2013a, 2014a, 2014b, 2017a, 2017b and 2017c).

Concomitantly, member states' governments and the Union cooperate (in a satisfactory way in most cases) towards achieving a functional coordination of social security schemes across the Union in order for workers to continue receiving pensions and social security benefits in the cases when they change a job and work in different member states (Europa, 2017; European Commission, 2016; Vasileiou, 2013a, 2014a, 2014b, 2017a, 2017b and 2017c).

We particularly emphasize the tremendous significance of the network of European employment services (EURES), one of the primary concerns of which is the best possible facilitation for a) companies to hire people from abroad and b) people to find jobs abroad (Europa, 2017; European Commission, 2016; Vasileiou, 2013a, 2014a, 2014b, 2017a, 2017b and 2017c).

Social security's proper coordination at Union level is a major issue, characterized by an enormous variety of significant economic as well as social implications. More specifically, the Union has indeed adopted common rules for the adequate protection of social security rights in the cases of moving within Europe (EU, Switzerland, Iceland, Norway and Liechtenstein) (European Commission/Coordination, 2017; Vasileiou, 2013a, 2014a, 2015 and 2017b).

It is emphatically highlighted that the rules in the context of social security coordination do not in any way replace national systems with a single European one. It is unambiguous that all countries without exception have the opportunity to take decisions regarding who can actually be insured under their legislation, the exact nature of specific benefits and the precise conditions (European Commission/Coordination, 2017; Vasileiou, 2013a, 2014a, 2015 and 2017b).

It goes without saying that such an issue is particularly critical for numerous important reasons and, therefore, the entire range of its (truly multidimensional) components must be seriously taken into consideration in order for present or future tribulations to be efficaciously avoided (European Commission/Coordination, 2017; Vasileiou, 2013a, 2014a, 2015 and 2017b).

According to official European Commission data, these rules apply to the following three categories of persons: a) nationals of the Union, Switzerland, Iceland, Norway or Liechtenstein, who are or used to be insured in the past in one of those countries, as well as their family members, b) refugees or stateless persons residing in the EU, Switzerland, Iceland, Norway or Liechtenstein and are or used to be in the past insured in one of those countries, and their family members and c) nationals of non-EU countries legally residing within the Union's territory, who have been moved between these countries, as well as their family members (European Commission/Coordination, 2017; Vasileiou, 2013a, 2014a, 2015 and 2017b).

We observe that the Union remains all but inactive on issues relating to unemployment, employment and social affairs. As with any economic policy issue that affects a large part of the population, it is natural for numerous different views to exist. This enormous variety we discover in terms of opinions and disagreements may well serve as a valuable basis towards a more constructive tomorrow (Alexiou, 2001; Bambra and Eikemo, 2009; Blanchflower and Shadforth, 2009; Calmfors, 2001; Christodoulakis and Mamatzakis, 2009; Daveri et al., 2000; Dieckhoff, 2011; Ederveen et al., 2007; Feld, 2005; Fialová and Schneider, 2009; Gobbin and Van Aarle, 2001; Heinrich and Hildebrand, 2005; Kazamaki Ottersten, 2004; Lipsmeyer and Zhu, 2011; Núñez and Livanos, 2010; Overman et al., 2002; Stanef, 2012; Stewart, 2005; Tatsiramos, 2009).

It is absolutely impossible for perfection to be found and much less when we refer to such complex issues, especially these days. What counts for us, though, is that the EU is continuously fighting for a better future and we truly hope that in the long run results will be regarded as even more successful.

In the following chapter, a critical analysis of the Union's funding programs in the context of employment and social affairs is being methodically presented. We meticulously focus on the European Social Fund, the European Globalization Adjustment Fund, the Fund for European Aid to the most Deprived and the "EU Programme for Employment and Social Innovation". Our objective is on the one hand to provide adequate information on quantitative data and on the other hand to draw a number of fruitful conclusions in terms of the programs' degree of effectiveness so far.

CHAPTER 2

EUROPEAN UNION FUNDING PROGRAMS FOR EMPLOYMENT AND SOCIAL AFFAIRS

In this chapter, EU funding programs for employment and social affairs are being rigorously examined. The funding issue is absolutely vital for the materialization of all kinds of strategies and policies, and that is why we are continuously delving into this specific issue.

As we will notice, the funding programs cover an enormous range of key issues, such as a) unemployment b) the consequences of globalization, c) poverty and d) social exclusion. These issues, apart from affecting a large part of the Union's population, somehow define the basic framework of almost all EU policies in the near future.

We assert with certainty that the Union is fully aware of both the existing problems and the precise notability of the decisions it is called upon to take. Many decisive steps have already taken place, but efforts in general must definitely continue with the same zeal (Alexiou, 2001; Bambra and Eikemo, 2009; Blanchflower and Shadforth, 2009; Calmfors, 2001; Christodoulakis and Mamatzakis, 2009; Daveri et al.,

2000; Dieckhoff, 2011; Ederveen et al., 2007; Feld, 2005; Fialová and Schneider, 2009; Gobbin and Van Aarle, 2001; Heinrich and Hildebrand, 2005; Kazamaki Ottersten, 2004; Lipsmeyer and Zhu, 2011; Núñez and Livanos, 2010; Overman et al., 2002; Stanef, 2012; Stewart, 2005; Tatsiramos, 2009).

The European Commission, in the context of its ongoing struggle for economic recovery, is financing numerous interesting projects in terms of employment, social protection and inclusion through the European Social Fund, the European Globalization Adjustment Fund, the Fund for European Aid to the most Deprived and the "EU Programme for Employment and Social Innovation" (European Commission/Funding, 2017).

Our analysis begins with the European Social Fund (ESF), which is considered to be the foremost instrument for supporting jobs and citizens in their efforts to find more satisfactory jobs. The primary concern of the ESF is to secure fairer job opportunities for all the Union citizens without exception. Such a component is outstandingly crucial especially nowadays (Brine, 2002; European Commission/ESF, 2013; Pratschke, 1981; Vasileiou, 2013a and 2014a; Welbers, 2011; Zamfir, 2011).

The ESF financing, which reaches €10 bn annually, aims towards the immediate enhancement in terms of job prospects of millions of citizens, expectedly placing emphasis on those who have difficulties in finding a job (Brine, 2002; European

Commission/ESF, 2013; European Commission/Funding, 2017; Pratschke, 1981; Vasileiou, 2013a and 2014a; Welbers, 2011; Zamfir, 2011).

In line with the Europe 2020 strategy, the EU is committed to the creation of more and better jobs, accompanied by a society lacking social exclusion. The outstandingly noteworthy pursuit of the coveted smart, sustainable and inclusive growth within the EU is a pivotal factor for both the present and the future of the Union and its citizens. The ESF contributes in practice, in its own unique way, to this objective, focusing on the reduction of unemployment and poverty wherever possible (Brine, 2002; European Commission/ESF, 2013; Pratschke, 1981; Vasileiou, 2013a and 2014a; Welbers, 2011; Zamfir, 2011).

The economic crisis, which has not yet been terminated, makes the already important role of the ESF even more significant. Its priorities in general, as well as the method according to which it spends its resources, are defined by the Commission in close cooperation with the Union's member states (Brine, 2002; European Commission/ESF, 2013; Pratschke, 1981; Vasileiou, 2013a and 2014a; Welbers, 2011; Zamfir, 2011).

More specifically, its priorities include a) the effective reinforcement of the adaptability of workers with new skills and of enterprises with new ways of working, b) the functional enhancement as regards access to employment, either by helping young people in the context of the (often problematic) transition from school to work, or by providing satisfactory assistance with regard to effective training for people with low skills who are looking for a job and c) the adequate assistance to people from disadvantaged groups in order to get a job (Brine, 2002; European Commission/ESF, 2013; Pratschke, 1981; Vasileiou, 2013a and 2014a; Welbers, 2011; Zamfir, 2011).

We incontrovertibly claim that burning issues such as social inclusion, vocational training and lifelong learning are fundamental elements in the context of the ESF's truly remarkable work (Brine, 2002; European Commission/ESF, 2013; European Commission/Funding, 2017; Pratschke, 1981; Vasileiou, 2013a and 2014a; Welbers, 2011; Zamfir, 2011).

Furthermore, attention must be paid to the fact that the ESF funds tens of thousands of national, regional and local employment-related projects throughout the Union (Brine, 2002; European Commission/ESF, 2013; European Commission/Funding, 2017; Pratschke, 1981; Vasileiou, 2013a and 2014a; Welbers, 2011; Zamfir, 2011).

The dominant objective of the European Globalization Adjustment Fund (EGF) is the provision of support to people who lose their jobs due to a) the global economic and financial crisis or b) structural changes occurring in global trade precisely because of globalization. We point out that EGF's maximum annual budget is €150 million for the period 2014-20 (Europa, 2017; European Commission/EGF, 2017; European

Commission/Funding, 2017; European Commission/Press Release Database, 2017; European Commission/Press Release Database/Employment, 2015).

The EGF has the possibility to fund up to 60% of the cost of projects set up for workers made redundant in order to assist them to find a new job or create their own business. Additional emphasis is placed on the fact that, as a rule, the EGF can solely be used in cases of dismissal of more than 500 employees by an individual company[2] or the dismissal of a large number of workers from a specific sector in one or more neighboring regions. Such an element must be seriously taken into consideration (European Commission/EGF, 2017; European Commission/Press Release Database, 2017; European Commission/Press Release Database/Employment, 2015).

Member states' national and regional authorities are in charge of not only the sufficient management but also the successful implementation of projects funded by the EGF. We must also mention that each project runs for two years (Europa, 2017; European Commission/EGF, 2017; European Commission/Press Release Database, 2017; European Commission/Press Release Database/Employment, 2015).

The EGF can actually co-finance specific projects which include measures such as a) entrepreneurship and business creation, b) assistance as far as job search is concerned,

---

2. *Also including both its suppliers and downstream producers.*

c) mentoring and coaching, d) advice relating to (the particularly thorny especially nowadays) career issues and e) education, training and retraining (Europa, 2017; European Commission/EGF, 2017; European Commission/Press Release Database, 2017; European Commission/Press Release Database/Employment, 2015).

As we can easily conclude, the EGF is spreading over an enormously wide range of issues, and such a fact unambiguously demonstrates its momentousness.

Additionally, the EGF can indeed provide a) training and mobility/relocation allowances, b) subsistence allowances or c) relevant forms of support. However, it is highlighted that the EGF does not co-finance social protection measures, such as unemployment benefit or pensions (Europa, 2017; European Commission/EGF, 2017; European Commission/ Press Release Database, 2017; European Commission/Press Release Database/Employment, 2015).

The question that (rather expectably) arises is precisely who are the beneficiaries of EGF projects. Beneficiaries are individual workers who have been made redundant. In particular, for the 2014-20 period beneficiaries can be a) temporary workers, b) self-employed and c) fixed-term workers (Europa, 2017; European Commission/EGF, 2017; European Commission/Press Release Database, 2017; European Commission/Press Release Database/Employment, 2015).

We must also highlight the fact that until the end of 2017, young people who were out of employment, education or training in regions characterized by high youth unemployment could receive support from the EGF equivalent to that of workers in these specific regions (Europa, 2017; European Commission/EGF, 2017; European Commission/Funding, 2017; European Commission/Press Release Database, 2017; European Commission/Press Release Database/Employment, 2015).

Another critical issue is that the EGF funds cannot be used to keep companies in business, or for issues such as their restructuring or modernization. Finally, we note that the EGF offers workers individual support for a limited period of time and only for once (Europa, 2017; European Commission/ EGF, 2017; European Commission/Funding, 2017; European Commission/Press Release Database, 2017; European Commission/Press Release Database/Employment, 2015).

The Fund for European Aid to the most Deprived (FEAD) aims to actively support the actions of the Union's member states to provide material assistance to the most deprived. The term "material assistance" precisely means the distribution of food, clothing and miscellaneous essential items for personal use such as soap, shampoo and shoes (European Commission/ FEAD, 2017; European Commission/Funding, 2017; European Commission/News, 2017).

At the same time, the material assistance provision must be incontrovertibly accompanied by certain social inclusion measures, such as appropriate support and guidance, with the aim of getting these people out of poverty as soon as possible. It is worth mentioning that national authorities can also support the provision of non-material assistance to the most deprived, seeking their rapid and effective integration into society (European Commission/FEAD, 2017; European Commission/News, 2017).

As regards FEAD's functioning in general, the Commission approves the national programs for the period 2014-20, under which national authorities take decisions on the assistance delivery via partner organizations, which in the majority are non-governmental. A similar approach already takes place for cohesion funds (European Commission/FEAD, 2017; European Commission/Funding, 2017; European Commission/News, 2017).

The Union's member states are indeed capable of choosing not only the exact type of assistance they wish to provide[3], but also the precise method of obtaining and distributing the items in question (European Commission/FEAD, 2017; European Commission/News, 2017).

As far as national authorities are concerned, we stress the fact that they can either buy food and other goods themselves and then forward them to the specific partner organizations, or fund the organizations in order for the latter to purchase the items themselves (European Commission/FEAD, 2017; European Commission/News, 2017).

---

3. *We mean food or basic material assistance, or even the combination of both.*

What is more, partner organizations that buy food or other goods themselves can distribute them directly or seek the assistance of other partner organizations (European Commission/FEAD, 2017; European Commission/Funding, 2017; European Commission/News, 2017).

It must be mentioned that partner organizations are non-governmental ones or public bodies carefully selected by national authorities according to specific criteria which have been set at national level (European Commission/FEAD, 2017; European Commission/Funding, 2017; European Commission/News, 2017).

Over the 2014-20 period, more than €3.8 bn[4] are earmarked for FEAD and such an amount is far from insignificant. Moreover, special attention must be paid to the fact that EU member states are to contribute at least 15% in national co-financing to their national program. Such a factor is of paramount significance and we can easily understand why (European Commission/FEAD, 2017; European Commission/ News, 2017).

In general, FEAD will provide assistance to the most deprived persons during their initial steps of their exit from social exclusion and poverty, covering their basic needs in the most efficient way so that they can find work or participate in a training course such as for example those supported by the ESF. We can easily understand the close relationship

---

4. *In real terms.*

and interdependence between FEAD and ESF in the context of the EU's ongoing struggle for a less problematic future (European Commission/FEAD, 2017; European Commission/ News, 2017).

The final step of our analysis in this chapter is the "EU Programme for Employment and Social Innovation" (EaSI), which is a key financing instrument at Union level to a) tackle poverty and social exclusion in a more direct manner, b) considerably enhance working conditions, c) systematically promote sustainable and quality employment and d) methodically ensure adequate social protection (EFTA, 2017; European Commission/EaSI, 2017; European Commission/ Funding, 2017; Microfinance, 2017).

We remain perfectly sure that these parameters unambiguously summarize EaSI's particular notability, since it is rightly regarded as one of the cornerstones for promoting employment and adequately tackling social exclusion (EFTA, 2017; European Commission/EaSI, 2017; European Commission/Funding, 2017; Microfinance, 2017).

The Commission directly manages EaSI, which includes the following three programs: a) PROGRESS, b) Progress Microfinance and c) EURES. We have to point out that during the period 2007-13 these three programs were managed separately, while from January 2014 they form the three EaSI's axes (EFTA, 2017; European Commission/EaSI, 2017; European Commission/Funding, 2017; Microfinance, 2017).

The PROGRESS axis (61% of the total budget) supports modernization in the context of both employment and social policy (EFTA, 2017; European Commission/EaSI, 2017; Microfinance, 2017).

The Microfinance and Social Entrepreneurship axis (21% of the total budget) supports exactly what its name implies, that is access to microfinance and social entrepreneurship which are vital components for a more heartening economic future. Finally, the EURES axis (18% of the total budget) supports job mobility. For the period 2014-20, the total budget reaches €919,469,000[5] (EFTA, 2017; European Commission/EaSI, 2017; Microfinance, 2017).

Should we wish to critically focus on EaSI's principal goals, we can categorize them as follows: a) a further support and encouragement in terms of the rational development of adequate social protection systems and labor market policies, b) the best possible enhancement of both availability and accessibility of microfinance for vulnerable groups and micro-enterprises, combined with a more functional improvement of access to finance for social enterprises, c) a more functional modernization as regards the Union's legislation and the simultaneous guarantee of its adequate application, d) the maximum strengthening in terms of "ownership" of the Union's objectives, combined with a concomitant coordination of actions not only at EU but also at national level, in the context of the particularly sensitive areas

---

5. *In 2013 prices.*

of employment, social inclusion and social affairs and e) a more sufficient promotion of the outstandingly significant geographical mobility and the reinforcement of employment opportunities via the proper development of an open labor market (EFTA, 2017; European Commission/EaSI, 2017; European Commission/ Funding, 2017; Microfinance, 2017).

Through our thus far conducted research, we remain fully convinced that EaSI actually operates in a rational way so as to successfully materialize all the abovementioned goals.

Furthermore, we must note that towards their faster realization, EaSI a) combats not only discriminations but also long-term unemployment, b) continuously battles poverty and social exclusion, c) systematically supports young people and gender equality, d) promotes by intensified methods a high level of quality and sustainable employment and e) ensures as much as possible a proper social protection (EFTA, 2017; European Commission/EaSI, 2017; European Commission/ Funding, 2017; Microfinance, 2017).

In the next chapter, we attempt to conduct a thorough examination of the actions of the European Parliament, the EU Council, the European Commission, the European Economic and Social Committee, the Committee of the Regions and the EIB in the context of employment and social affairs.

The fundamental objective of our analysis is to facilitate the reader's understanding in terms of an exceedingly wide range of roles and tasks.

We truly hope that the method on which we have relied will provide substantial assistance towards the simplification of the outstandingly complex spectrum of the policies described, without, however, omitting basic parameters and details that are absolutely essential for further research.

CHAPTER 3

THE FOREMOST EUROPEAN UNION INSTITUTIONS AND BODIES FOR EMPLOYMENT AND SOCIAL AFFAIRS

In the context of this chapter, the responsibilities of the European Parliament, the Council of the EU, the European Commission, the European Economic and Social Committee, the Committee of the Regions and the EIB in the field of employment and social affairs are being critically discussed.

The starting point of our analysis is the European Parliament's Committee on Employment and Social Affairs (EMPL), which focuses not only on employment policies, but also on all the aspects of working conditions, vocational training, social policy and the free movement of workers and pensioners (Europa, 2017; European Parliament, 2017; Vasileiou, 2013a, 2014a, and 2017b).

EMPL consists of 55 members, representing the Parliament's various political groups. What is more, the rational EMPL operation is guaranteed both by the Chair and the four vice-Chairs and the coordinators appointed by political groups (Europa, 2017; European Parliament, 2017).

EMPL performs a close and constructive cooperation with the Council and the European Commission, as well as with miscellaneous institutions and representatives of civil society in order to determine the legislative framework in the areas within its competence (Europa, 2017; European Parliament, 2017; Vasileiou, 2013a, 2014a and 2017b).

These include a) combating unemployment (especially among young people) and precarious jobs, b) addressing in an efficacious manner the so-called "situations of abuse", such as the "circumvention" of laws designed for employees' protection and undeclared work and c) a rapid and substantial enhancement with regard to the rules on health and safety at work (Europa, 2017; European Parliament, 2017).

We argue that the examination of the multifunctional role of the EMPL highlights once more the Parliament's tremendous noteworthiness in the context of such issues.

The fundamental pursuits of the overall work of the EPSCO Council are a) to substantially improve both living and working conditions in the EU, b) to raise employment levels in the Union and c) to ensure an indeed high level of human health and consumer protection in the EU as fast as possible (European Council/Council of the European Union, 2017; Vasileiou, 2013a, 2014a and 2017b).

As its name suggests, the EPSCO Council brings together ministers in charge of employment, health, social affairs and consumer policy from all member states without exception. It is also stressed that the relevant European Commissioners also take part in the meetings (European Council/Council of the European Union, 2017; Vasileiou, 2013a, 2014a and 2017b).

The EPSCO Council usually carries out four meetings a year, and it must be noted that generally two of them exclusively concern employment and social policy issues. What is more, we highlight the fact that in the context of employment and social policy areas, the Council is responsible for the effective drawing up of the annual employment guidelines that member states take into account in terms of their national policies. Such a parameter incontrovertibly deserves particular attention (Europa, 2017; European Council/Council of the European Union, 2017; Vasileiou, 2013a, 2014a and 2017b).

Apart from that, the Council, together with the Parliament, adopts legislation on a) gender equality and b) the most satisfactory improvement in terms of working conditions and the adequate promotion and enhancement in terms of social inclusion (Europa, 2017; European Council/Council of the European Union, 2017).

Concurrently, it is stressed that, while member states retain full responsibility for defining their health policies and for organizing and providing healthcare, the Council, together with the Parliament, adopts legislation on a) the exact rights of patients with regard to cross-border healthcare and b) the safety and quality of human organs, blood, medicines and medical devices (European Council/Council of the European

Union, 2017; Vasileiou, 2013a, 2014a and 2017b).

Finally, in terms of consumer protection, the Council, again together with the Parliament adopts rules at Union level to protect not only the health and safety of consumers, but also their economic interests (Europa, 2017; European Council/ Council of the European Union, 2017; Vasileiou, 2013a, 2014a and 2017b).

The Section for Employment, Social Affairs and Citizenship (SOC) is responsible for the rational preparation of the work of the European Economic and Social Committee in the broader context of a wide range of key policy areas, such as a) education and training, b) employment, combined with working conditions, c) migration and asylum, d) fundamental and citizens' rights, e) poverty and social policy, f) disability issues, g) gender equality issues, h) Roma inclusion, i) health, j) justice and k) home affairs including immigration (Europa, 2017; European Economic and Social Committee, 2017).

Furthermore, it is worth noting that the most notable actions of the SOC Section include a) the future of work, b) the European Pillar of Social Rights and accompanying measures, and c) its overall work as far as migration and asylum are concerned (European Economic and Social Committee, 2017; Vasileiou, 2013a, 2014a and 2017b).

Simultaneously, the SOC Section is in charge of providing the secretariat for the European Migration Forum, which is organized by the European Economic and Social Committee together with the European Commission (European Economic and Social Committee, 2017; Vasileiou, 2013a, 2014a and 2017b).

The Commission for Economic Policy (ECON) is responsible for the proper coordination of the work of the Committee of the Regions in seven of the most neuralgic areas for both the present and the future of the Union. These are a) Economic and Monetary Policy, b) Industrial Policy, c) the Internal Market, d) SME policy, e) International Trade and Tariffs, f) Competition and State aid policy and g) Economic Governance, European Semester. The particular notability of these areas undoubtedly demonstrates ECON's paramount significance (CoR Commissions, 2017; Vasileiou, 2013a, 2014a and 2017b).

The EIB and the European Investment Fund are rightly considered to be absolutely pivotal factors, especially with regard to SMEs, which account for over 90% of businesses in the Union (Europa, 2017; European Commission, 2016; European Investment Bank, 2017; Vasileiou, 2013a, 2014a and 2017b).

It is remarkable that in 2016 alone, the EIB Group managed to finance SMEs and Midcaps around the globe with €33.6 bn. Moreover, it supported 300,000 smaller companies, employing 4.4 million people. Such a staggering feature must under no circumstances go unnoticed (Europa, 2017; European Commission, 2016; European Investment Bank, 2017; Vasileiou, 2013a, 2014a and 2017b).

What is more, the EIB Group focuses in a functional way on the development of innovative products and partnerships, which are unquestionably characterized by their ability to provide influential assistance regarding the coveted facilitation to access to finance for SMEs and Midcaps in the context of all their development stages (Europa, 2017; European Commission, 2016; European Investment Bank, 2017).

These actions incontrovertibly reveal a highly satisfactory organization that makes us optimistic despite the (inevitable) difficulties. We have repeatedly pointed out that in terms of such sensitive matters, the best possible coordination, accompanied by an emphasis on detail, are fundamental parameters should we wish to witness positive outcomes.

Through our hitherto conducted research, we are fully convinced that the EIB and the European Investment Fund together form an irresistible combination in the context of numerous truly valuable efforts to mobilize not only financial but also technical expertise. These can eventually become the catalyst for investment towards the pursuit of smart, sustainable and inclusive growth, which is absolutely essential especially nowadays (European Commission, 2016; European Investment Bank, 2017).

Furthermore, a) the European Insurance and Occupational Pensions Authority (EIOPA), b) the "European Centre for the Development of Vocational Training" (Cedefop), c) the European Agency for Safety and Health at Work (EU-

OSHA), d) the European Training Foundation (ETF) and e) the European Foundation for the Improvement of Living and Working Conditions (Eurofound) play a vital role in terms of employment and social affairs (Europa, 2017).

In the following (and final) chapter, the foremost points of our research are being methodically summarized, in order for a number of conclusions to be effectively drawn.

Unemployment, coupled with the economic crisis, are key regulatory factors for the EU and its member states (Alexiou, 2001; Bambra and Eikemo, 2009; Blanchflower and Shadforth, 2009; Calmfors, 2001; Christodoulakis and Mamatzakis, 2009; Daveri et al., 2000; Dieckhoff, 2011; Ederveen et al., 2007; Feld, 2005; Fialová and Schneider, 2009; Gobbin and Van Aarle, 2001; Heinrich and Hildebrand, 2005; Kazamaki Ottersten, 2004; Lipsmeyer and Zhu, 2011; Mahler et al., 2000; Núñez and Livanos, 2010; Overman et al., 2002; Stanef, 2012; Stewart, 2005; Sweeney, 1994; Tatsiramos, 2009) and we remain optimistic that the reader is now capable of conducting his own assessment regarding the Union's overall actions in the wider context of employment and social affairs.

CHAPTER 4

CONCLUDING REMARKS

Following our hitherto conducted analysis, we strongly believe that we are capable of drawing a number of interesting conclusions that, in our opinion, effectively summarize the foremost points.

As we have noticed in the previous chapters, the unemployment issue is characterized by numerous critical aspects and consequences. Initiatives and actions which are directly or indirectly associated with it require a systematic organization, emphasis on detail and (without exaggeration) "surgical precision" actions, especially at this period when the Union is struggling to overcome the crisis.

The areas linked to unemployment, such as economic growth, globalization, regional disparities, taxation, education, crime, labor market reforms, industrial restructuring, migration, social welfare and the role of domestic political institutions are vital for the Union's entire population. Hence, it is only natural that numerous scholars and authors worldwide have been engaged in extensive research on these sectors.

The unemployment issue with its various sociopolitical and economic implications could well be described as inexhaustible, but in the context of this book we decided to concentrate on a number of specific points. According to the EU, solutions for combating unemployment and miscellaneous tribulations in the wider context of social protection and inclusion indeed exist. However, in order for them to eventually become a reality, certain conditions must definitely apply.

Both the investment plan for Europe and the EFSI have been remarkable initiatives that have unambiguously demonstrated that the Union is operating in a rapid and systematic way to fight the crisis, revitalize investment, promote quality market reforms and functionally implement appropriate financial policies in order to avoid a public debt beyond control.

Furthermore, we hope that the analysis of Ginkgo Fund 2, the European Investment Advisory Hub and the European Investment Project Portal can convince even the most skeptical that the EU is constantly trying to upgrade its overall strategies and policies towards the fastest possible investment and economic recovery, which these days is perhaps more essential than ever.

Moreover, the European Structural and Investment Funds play their own unique role towards the desirable immediate reversal of the crisis' negative impact.

A further delving into the EGF, the FEAD and the EaSI responsibilities was absolutely indispensable, given the pivotal roles they play in terms of the Union efforts to adequately tackle problems related to globalization, unemployment, poverty and social exclusion.

The scrutiny of the tasks of the European Parliament, the Council of the EU, the European Commission, the European Economic and Social Committee, the Committee of the Regions and the EIB in the context of employment and social affairs, make us understand their momentousness which stems from the substantial assistance they provide in terms of the continuous fight against the crisis.

As we noticed in Chapter 3, numerous noteworthy Union bodies, such as EIOPA, Cedefop, EU-OSHA, ETF and Eurofound are intensively engaged in several important issues in the context of employment and social affairs.

In general, the range of institutions and agencies dealing with these issues is extremely broad and the Union's ability to combine their functions wherever needed is indubitably admirable. We argue beyond any doubt that, despite the complexity and all inevitable difficulties, both the organization and the overall coordination are at a tremendously high level.

Once again, time will judge the efficiency of policies, while it is unambiguous that all sorts of unpredictable factors in the near or distant future are virtually impossible to calculate. Nonetheless, research findings literally oblige us to stress the continuous and consistent struggle of the Union for a more optimistic tomorrow for the current and the future generations.

BIBLIOGRAPHY

Alexiou, Constantinos (2001), "Crafting a Post-Keynesian Macroeconomic Framework to Explain European Unemployment: Econometric Evidence from the European Union Countries", *Journal of Post Keynesian Economics*, 24 (1), pp. 59-80.

Bambra, C. and Eikemo, T.A. (2009), "Welfare state regimes, unemployment and health: a comparative study of the relationship between unemployment and self-reported health in 23 European countries", *Journal of Epidemiology and Community Health (1979-)*, 63 (2), pp. 92-98.

Bartolomew, David, Moore, Peter, Smith, Fred and Allin, Paul (1995), "The Measurement of Unemployment in the UK", *Journal of the Royal Statistical Society. Series A (Statistics in Society)*, 158 (3), pp. 363-417.

Blanchflower, David G. and Shadforth, Chris (2009), "Fear, Unemployment and Migration", *The Economic Journal*, 119 (535), pp. F136-F182.

Brine, Jacky (2002), "Further Education Participation, European Expansion and European Erasure", *British Educational Research Journal*, 28 (1), pp.21-36.

Calmfors, Lars (2001), "Unemployment, Labor Market Reform and Monetary Union", *Journal of Labor Economics*, 19 (2), pp. 265-289.

Christodoulakis, G.A and Mamatzakis, E.C. (2009), "Assessing the Prudence of Economic Forecasts in the EU", *Journal of Applied Econometrics*, 24 (4), pp. 583-606.

Coombes, Mike and Raybould, Simon (2004), "Finding Work in 2001: Urban-Rural Contrasts across England in Employment Rates and Local Job Availability", *Area*, 36 (2), pp. 202-222.

CoR Commissions (2017), "Commission for Economic Policy (ECON)" (in Greek), available at http://cor.europa.eu/el/activities/commissions/Pages/cor-commissions.aspx?comm=ECON (accessed on 3/10/17).

BIBLIOGRAPHY

Daveri, Francesco, Tabellini, Guido, Bentolila, Samuel and Huizinga, Harry (2000), "Unemployment, Growth and Taxation in Industrial Countries", *Economic Policy*, 15 (30), pp. 47-104.

Dieckhoff, Martina (2011), "The effect of unemployment on subsequent job quality in Europe: A comparative study of four countries", *Acta Sociologica*, 54 (3), pp. 233-249.

Ederveen, Sjef, Nahuis, Richard and Parikh, Ashok (2007), "Labour Mobility and Regional Disparities: The Role of Female Labour Participation", *Journal of Population Economics*, 20 (4), pp. 895-913.

EFTA (2017), "Programme for Employment and Social Innovation", Home-European Economic Area (EEA)/Relations with the EU-EU Programmes with EEA EFTA Participation-Programme for Employment and Social Innovation (EaSI), available at http://www.efta.int/eea/eu-programmes/employment-and-social-innovation (accessed on 25/10/17).

Europa (2017), "Employment and social affairs" (in Greek), available at https://europa.eu/european-union/topics/employment-social-affairs_el (accessed on 23/9/17).

European Commission (2016), "The EU and Jobs, Growth and Investment" (in Greek), EU Law and Publications, October 2016, available at https://publications.europa.eu/el/publication-detail/-/publication/b9ac1176-9a88-11e6-9bca-01aa75ed71a1 (accessed on 23/9/17).

European Commission/Coordination (2017), "Employment, social affairs and social inclusion/EU social security coordination" (in Greek), available at http://ec.europa.eu/social/main.jsp?langId=el&catId=849 (accessed on 6/10/17).

BIBLIOGRAPHY

European Commission/EaSI (2017), "EU Programme for Employment and Social Innovation (EaSI)" (in Greek), available at http://ec.europa.eu/social/main.jsp?catId=1081&langId=el (accessed on 28/9/17).

European Commission/EGF (2017), "European Globalization Adjustment Fund (EGF)" (in Greek), available at http://ec.europa.eu/social/main.jsp?catId=326&langId=el (accessed on 28/9/17).

European Commission/ESF (2013), "European Social Fund-What is the ESF?" (in Greek), available at http://ec.europa.eu/esf/main.jsp?catId=35&langId=el (accessed on 28/9/17).

European Commission/FEAD (2017), "Fund for European Aid to the Most Deprived (FEAD)" (in Greek), available at http://ec.europa.eu/social/main.jsp?catId=1089&langId=el (accessed on 28/9/17).

European Commission/Funding (2017), "Employment, social affairs and social inclusion/Funding" (in Greek), available at http://ec.europa.eu/social/main.jsp?catId=86&langId=el (accessed on 4/10/17).

European Commission/News (2017), "Fund for European aid to the most deprived helped 14 million people in 2015", available at http://ec.europa.eu/social/main.jsp?langId=el&catId=89&newsId=2855 (accessed on 24/10/17).

European Commission/Policies and activities (2017), "Employment, social affairs and social inclusion/Policies and Activities" (in Greek), available at http://ec.europa.eu/social/main.jsp?langId=el&catId=1 (accessed on 4/10/17).

European Commission/Press Release Database (2017), "Ten years of European solidarity via the European Globalisation Adjustment Fund", available at http://europa.eu/rapid/press-release_IP-17-443_en.htm (accessed on 24/10/17).

BIBLIOGRAPHY

European Commission/Press Release Database/Employment
(2015), "Employment: Almost 30,000 workers supported
by the European Globalisation Adjustment Fund during
2013 and 2014", available at http://europa.eu/rapid/press-
release_IP-15-5412_en.htm (accessed on 24/10/17).

European Commission/Social Protection and Social Inclusion (2017),
"Employment, social affairs and social inclusion/Social Protection
and Social Inclusion" (in Greek), available at http://ec.europa.eu/
social/main.jsp?langId=el&catId=750 (accessed on 6/10/17).

European Council/Council of the European Union (2017),
"Employment, Social Policy, Health and Consumer Affairs Council
configuration (EPSCO)" (in Greek), available at http://www.consilium.
europa.eu/el/council-eu/configurations/epsco/ (accessed on 2/10/17).

European Economic and Social Committee (2017), "Section
for Employment, Social Affairs and Citizenship (SOC)" (in
Greek), available at http://www.eesc.europa.eu/el/sections-
other-bodies/sections-commission/employment-social-
affairs-and-citizenship-soc (accessed on 3/10/17).

European Investment Bank (2017), "SMEs and Midcaps",
available at http://www.eib.org/projects/priorities/
sme/index.htm?lang=en (accessed on 5/10/17).

European Parliament (2017), "Committees/Employment
and Social Affairs (EMPL)" (Thomas Händel) (in Greek),
available at http://www.europarl.europa.eu/committees/
el/empl/home.html (accessed on 2/10/17).

Feld, Lars P. (2005), "The European Constitution Project
from the Perspective of Constitutional Political
Economy", *Public Choice*, 122 (3/4), pp. 417-448.

BIBLIOGRAPHY

Fialová, Kamila and Schneider, Ondřej (2009), "Labor
Market Institutions and Their Effect on Labor Market
Performance in the New EU Member Countries",
Eastern European Economics, 47 (3), pp. 57-83.

Fragoulis, Haralabos, Masson, Jean-Raymond and Klenha, Vaclav
(2004), "Improving Opportunities for Adult Learning in the
Acceding and Candidate Countries of Central and Eastern
Europe", *European Journal of Education*, 39 (1), pp. 9-30.

Gobbin, Niko and Van Aarle, Bas (2001), "Fiscal
Adjustments and Their Effects during the Transition to
the EMU", *Public Choice*, 109 (3/4), pp. 269-299.

Heinrich, Georges and Hildebrand, Vincent (2005), "Returns
to Education in the European Union: A Reassessment from
Comparative Data", *European Journal of Education*, 40 (1), pp. 13-34.

Janáčková, Stanislava (1998), "Convergence for European
Union Accession: Challenges for Czech Monetary Policy",
Eastern European Economics, 36 (3), pp. 80-95.

Kazamaki Ottersten, Eugenia (2004), "Lifelong Learning
and Challenges Posed to European Labour Markets",
European Journal of Education, 39 (2), pp. 151-159.

Kinsella, Ray and Kinsella, Maurice (2011), "The rise and rise of
long term and youth unemployment in Ireland: the scarring of a
generation", Studies: *An Irish Quarterly Review*, 100 (397), pp. 83-102.

Kogan, Irena (2004), "Last Hired, First Fired? The
Unemployment Dynamics of Male Immigrants in Germany",
European Sociological Review, 20 (5), pp. 445-461.

BIBLIOGRAPHY

Kogan, Irena (2006), "Labor Markets and Economic Incorporation among Recent Immigrants in Europe", *Social Forces,* 85 (2), pp. 697-721.

Lipsmeyer, Christine S. and Zhu, Ling (2011), "Immigration, Globalization, and Unemployment Benefits in Developed EU States", *American Journal of Political Science,* 55 (3), pp. 647-664.

Mahler, Vincent A., Taylor, Bruce J and Wozniak, Jennifer R. (2000), "Economics and Public Support for the European Union: An Analysis at the National, Regional and Individual Levels", *Polity,* 32 (3), pp. 429-453.

Microfinance (2017), "TA under the EU Programme for Employment and Social Innovation (EaSI)", Microfinance Centre/Current Projects, available at http://mfc.org.pl/technical-assistance-for-employment-and-social-innovation/ (accessed on 25/10/17).

Newell, Andrew and Pastore, Francesco (2006), "Regional Unemployment and Industrial Restructuring in Poland", *Eastern European Economics,* 44 (3), pp. 5-28.

Núñez, Imanol and Livanos, Ilias (2010), "Higher education and unemployment in Europe: an analysis of the academic subject and national effects", *Higher Education,* 59 (4), pp. 475-487.

Öster, Anna and Agell, Jonas (2007), "Crime and Unemployment in Turbulent Times", *Journal of the European Economic Association,* 5 (4), pp. 752-775.

Overman, Henry G., Puga, Diego and Vandenbussche, Hylke (2002), "Unemployment Clusters across Europe's Regions and Countries", *Economic Policy,* 17 (34), pp. 115-147.

BIBLIOGRAPHY

Palazuelos-Martinez, Manuel (2007), "The Structure and
Evolution of Trade in Central and Eastern Europe in the
1990s", *Europe-Asia Studies*, 59 (1), pp. 111-135.

Pelagidis, Theodore and Mitsopoulos, Michael (2014), *Greece-From
Exit to Recovery?* (Washington D.C.: Brookings Institution Press).

Petrongolo, Barbara and Pissarides, Christopher A. (2008),
"The Ins and Outs of European Unemployment", *The
American Economic Review*, 98 (2), pp. 256-262.

Pollmann-Schult, Matthias and Büchel, Felix (2005), "Unemployment
Benefits, Unemployment Duration and Subsequent Job Quality:
Evidence from West Germany", *Acta Sociologica*, 48 (1), pp. 21-39.

Pratschke, John L. (1981), "Rural and Farm Dwellings in
the European Community", *Irish Journal of Agricultural
Economics and Rural Sociology*, 8 (2), pp. 191-211.

Scott, Peter J. and Kelleher, Michael (1996), "Convergence
and Fragmentation? Vocational Training within the EU",
European Journal of Education, 31 (4), pp. 463-481.

Smith, Jennifer C. (2011), "The Ins and Outs of UK Unemployment",
The Economic Journal, 121 (552), pp. 402-444.

Stanef, Mihaela Roberta (2012), "Measuring Differences in Urban-
Rural Development: The Case of Unemployment", *Theoretical
and Empirical Researches in Urban Management*, 7 (3), pp. 44-52.

Stewart, Kitty (2005), "Dimensions of Well-Being in EU
Regions: Do GDP and Unemployment Tell Us All We Need
To Know?", *Social Indicators Research*, 73 (2), pp. 221-246.

BIBLIOGRAPHY

Sweeney, John (1994), "On Bringing in the Outsiders: What
Price Solidarity with the Long-Term Unemployed?", *Studies:
An Irish Quarterly Review*, 83 (331), pp. 265-275.

Tatsiramos, Konstantinos (2009), "Unemployment Insurance in Europe:
Unemployment Duration and Subsequent Employment Stability",
Journal of the European Economic Association, 7 (6), pp. 1225-1260.

Vasileiou, Ioannis (2013a), *European Unification-A Process of
Convergence, or Divergence?* (in Greek) (Athens: Historical Quest).

Vasileiou, Ioannis (2013b), "1980-1999, European Union: The Years of
Expansion and Enlargement", *From Hitler's New Europe to Merkel's
Eurozone* (in Greek), Vol. 1, Historical Archive of Ependytis, pp. 76-95.

Vasileiou, Ioannis (2014a), *European Unification-A Process
of Convergence, or Divergence?* (2nd Edition-Special Edition
for Universities) (in Greek) (Athens: Historical Quest).

Vasileiou, Ioannis (2014b), *The Present and Future of the Agricultural
Policy of the European Union* (in Greek) (Athens: Historical Quest).

Vasileiou, Ioannis (2015), *The Foreign and Security Policy of the European
Union-A Critical Approach* (in Greek) (Athens: Historical Quest).

Vasileiou, Ioannis (2017a), *Climate Change: Manageable Problem or
Slow Death of the Planet? Role and Actions of the EU until 2050-
The impact on Greece* (in Greek) (Athens: Historical Quest).

Vasileiou, Ioannis (2017b), *EU Budget-Issues about
the Allocation and Redistribution of Resources in the
EU* (in Greek) (Athens: Historical Quest).

Vasileiou, Ioannis (2017c), *European Union and Energy-
The Route Towards 2050-Thoughts, Ideas and Conclusions*
(in Greek) (Athens: Historical Quest).

BIBLIOGRAPHY

Vasileiou, Ioannis (2017d), *The European Union Expansion Into Space* (in Greek) (Athens: Historical Quest).

Vintrová, Růžena (2004), "The CEE Countries on the Way into the EU: Adjustment Problems: Institutional Adjustment, Real and Nominal Convergence", *Europe-Asia Studies*, 56 (4), pp. 521-541.

Walsh, Brendan (2000), "Cyclical and Structural Influences on Irish Employment", *Oxford Economic Papers*, 52 (1), pp. 119-145.

Welbers, Gerhard (2011), "The European Social Fund: changing approaches to VET", *European Journal of Education*, 46 (1), pp. 54-69.

Zamfir, Andreea Ileana (2011), "Management of Renewable Energy and Regional Development: European Experiences and Steps Forward", *Theoretical and Empirical Researches in Urban Management*, 6 (3), pp. 35-42.

IOANNIS VASILEIOU

BIOGRAPHY

Ioannis Vasileiou was born in Athens in 1978. In 2001, he was awarded his Ptychio (equivalent to Bachelor's degree) in Political Science and Public Administration from the University of Athens (Greece). In 2003, he was awarded his first Master's degree (International Political Economy) from the University of Warwick (UK). In 2005, he was awarded his second Master's degree (International Economic Management) from the University of Birmingham (UK). In 2011, he was awarded his PhD from the University of Birmingham (UK) with specialization in the economic and political aspects of the European Union's Regional Policy. Since 2011, he has been conducting academic research on issues related to the European Union and international politics and economics.